CHILDREN'S AUTHORS

GARY PAULSEN

Jill C. Wheeler

Checkerboard
Library

An Imprint of Abdo Publishing
www.abdopublishing.com

www.abdopublishing.com

Published by Abdo Publishing, a division of ABDO, PO Box 398166, Minneapolis, Minnesota 55439. Copyright © 2015 by Abdo Consulting Group, Inc. International copyrights reserved in all countries. No part of this book may be reproduced in any form without written permission from the publisher. Checkerboard Library™ is a trademark and logo of Abdo Publishing.

Printed in the United States of America, North Mankato, Minnesota.
102014
012015

THIS BOOK CONTAINS
RECYCLED MATERIALS

Cover Photo: AP Images
Interior Photos: AP Images pp. 5, 9, 13, 15, 17, 21; Corbis p. 19; iStockphoto pp. 7, 11

Series Coordinator: Bridget O'Brien
Editors: Rochelle Baltzer, Megan M. Gunderson
Art Direction: Neil Klinepier

Library of Congress Cataloging-in-Publication Data

Wheeler, Jill C., 1964-
 Gary Paulsen / Jill C. Wheeler.
      pages cm. -- (Children's Authors)
 Includes bibliographical references and index.
 ISBN 978-1-62403-668-2
1. Paulsen, Gary--Juvenile literature. 2. Authors, American--20th century--Biography--Juvenile literature. 3. Young adult fiction--Authorship--Juvenile literature. I. Title.
 PS3566.A834Z94 2015
 813'.54--dc23
 [B]
                              2014025379

CONTENTS

Literary Crusader

Gary Paulsen thinks everyone should love reading. For more than 40 years, he has worked to spread that love among even the most reluctant readers. Paulsen believes everything people are is locked up in books. If a person cannot read those books, then all of that is lost.

More than 26 million copies of Paulsen's books are in print. Paulsen is a favorite author of many people, especially boys who do not typically like to read. His work has been recognized with three **Newbery Honors**.

Paulsen never set out to become a writer. However, he has written for several audiences. In addition to his novels, Paulsen is the author of several picture books. He also has written children's nonfiction titles and two plays. And, he writes fiction and nonfiction books and magazine articles for adults.

Most of Paulsen's work is inspired by his own adventures. He is an experienced hunter and trapper. He has driven more than 27,000 miles (43,450 km) on a dogsled. He has also sailed across the Pacific Ocean twice.

Paulsen is careful to note that he does not go on adventures simply to write about them. But, he does love to write about his adventures after he has them!

Aside from being an award-winning author, Paulsen has worked as a teacher, farmer, singer, sculptor, and sailor.

"UGLY" CHILDHOOD

Gary Paulsen was born on May 17, 1939, in Minneapolis, Minnesota. His parents were first-generation **immigrants**. His father's parents were from Denmark. His mother's parents came from Norway and Sweden. Gary had an older sister, Paulette, and a half brother, Bill.

Gary's father, Oscar, was an officer in the US Army. He was serving in **World War II** when Gary was born. While Oscar was fighting, Gary and his mother, Eunice, lived in Chicago, Illinois. She worked at an **ammunition** factory.

When World War II ended, Gary was seven. Eunice took him on a ship across the Pacific Ocean to meet Oscar. The Paulsens reunited in the Philippines.

The family lived in Manila, Philippines, for three years. Gary recalls those years as hard. Both of his parents had issues with alcohol. Gary felt lonely.

Minneapolis, Minnesota

Things improved little when the family returned to the United States. After briefly living in Washington, DC, they returned to northern Minnesota. There, Gary was shy and had few friends. His parents were still drinking heavily. Gary was unpopular and poor at sports. He also struggled in school. He recalls his childhood as nothing short of "ugly."

KINDNESS & A LIBRARY CARD

Fortunately, not all of Gary's childhood was ugly. He had a grandmother, aunts, uncles, and cousins in Minnesota. They helped provide some of the stability he lacked at home. Gary's relatives owned farms. In the summer, Gary worked on their farms.

Gary found comfort in nature. He learned to hunt, trap, and fish. Sometimes, Gary would spend nights or even weekends in the woods. Other times, he would skip an entire week of school.

As a teen, Gary took jobs selling newspapers and setting pins at a bowling alley. He also joined a carnival for a bit. One summer, Gary worked in the sugar beet fields of North Dakota.

Gary's life changed one freezing winter night when he was 14. While walking past the public library, he decided to go inside and warm up. He was surprised when the librarian asked if he wanted a library card. She also

Gary went on to write **Tiltawhirl John** *and* **Sentries** *about his adventures working in the sugar beet fields.*

recommended books she thought he would enjoy.

Within minutes, Gary had a library card. It was the first time he had ever had anything with his name on it. The card opened a window to a new world. Gary devoured the titles the librarian recommended, including science fiction, westerns, and classics. He never forgot her kindness or how reading changed his life.

MINDING MISSILES

Even though he loved reading, Gary struggled in school. He had skipped so many classes that he did not pass ninth grade. He had to do most of ninth and tenth grades together in order to finish school on time. Gary barely graduated from Lincoln High School in Thief River Falls, Minnesota, in 1957. His final grades were mostly Ds.

Gary had spent much of his youth outdoors. He used his hunting and trapping skills to earn money for college. He put himself through two years of pre-engineering studies at Bemidji College in Bemidji, Minnesota.

Then in 1959, Gary joined the US Army. A tough drill sergeant forced Gary to see his life needed to change. Gary began working hard. He entered the army's missile program.

Gary left the army in May 1962. Then, he took courses to become an electronics engineer. For three years, he worked tracking satellites for **aerospace** companies. He was good at the work, yet he did not enjoy it. By that time, he was also married with two children, Lance and Lynn. But, the marriage ended in divorce when he was 26.

    One day after reading a magazine article, Gary was inspired to change his job. It struck him that there were people who made a living by writing. He decided if they could do it, so could he. Gary quit his job that day. He headed to Hollywood, California, to become a writer.

Gary hunted destructive animals, such as coyotes, to earn money for college.

Writer in Training

Paulsen knew a lot about engineering, but not much about writing for a living. In California, he decided he would learn by getting a job at a magazine. After creating a fake **résumé**, he sent it to the editor of a magazine publishing company.

Soon, Paulsen was hired to work on a men's magazine. His new employer quickly realized the résumé had been fake. Yet he saw Paulsen had talent, so he kept him on the staff. Other staff members helped Paulsen learn about writing, editing, and page layout.

Writing was just one opportunity Paulsen found in California. He lived on a sailboat in Ventura Harbor. He worked as an **extra** on movie sets. He briefly took up wood sculpting and even won a prize. He also married for a second time.

Yet Paulsen quickly tired of Hollywood. And, his marriage ended. He moved back to Minnesota. Paulsen lived in a cabin that he rented for $25 a month. There in the north woods, he kept writing.

Paulsen's first book, *The Special War*, was published in 1966. It came from material Paulsen gathered interviewing soldiers returning from the **Vietnam War**.

Paulsen finds inspiration for his books from nature and his own experiences. He also likes to write about his dogs.

HITTING BOTTOM

After becoming a published author, Paulsen moved again. He lived in California for a short time. In late 1967, he moved to Taos, New Mexico. He wanted to join the local community of artists and writers.

One of those artists was Ruth Wright. She and Paulsen began dating and moved to Colorado in 1969. Two years later, they married and had a son, James. He went by Jim.

In 1969, Paulsen had published *Mr. Tucket*, his first novel for young adults. It is part of a series about a young boy who leaves his family during their journey on the **Oregon Trail**. The boy ends up living with Native Americans.

Meanwhile in Colorado, Paulsen drifted from job to job. He worked in roofing, tree cutting, and construction, among other things. He struggled to keep jobs because he had started drinking in New Mexico.

Paulsen's alcohol problem got worse. He was worried he was putting his young son in danger. He decided to stop drinking. And with help, he did just that.

Finally, Paulsen got back to writing. He spent two years working to find his writing voice again. At one point, he almost gave up. Then, he began churning out nonfiction books for kids and adults on topics from biographies to sports. In 1976, he published his young adult novel *Winterkill*.

Once on a bet with a friend, Paulsen wrote 11 articles and short stories in just four days. He sold every one of them!

BACK TO NATURE

Paulsen's career took a turn in 1979. He was **sued** for **libel** based on the book *Winterkill*. Paulsen won his court case. But later, he was not paid for a book contract. Paulsen was in **debt** and tired of publishing. He and his family returned to Minnesota. They lived in a rough home with no indoor plumbing.

Paulsen decided to return to one of his old skills, trapping predators. A friend sold Paulsen a team of dogs. Shortly after getting the dogs, Paulsen stayed out in the woods with them for seven days. He was enchanted by the dogs, the landscape, and how everything worked together.

Paulsen had found a new passion. Dogsledding made him realize he did not want to trap again. It was time to go back to writing. He collected new material for his work in 1983. At that time, he entered a famous sled dog race called the Iditarod.

Paulsen ran his dogs for 17 days in a row with no sleep. He came in forty-second out of a field of 73 **mushers**. His book

The Iditarod race is more than 1,000 miles (1,600 km) long. It is run in Alaska, from Anchorage to Nome. Contestants run their dogs in bitter cold and blizzard conditions.

Winterdance is the story of his experiences on the trail with his dogs. The Iditarod also appears in his book *Woodsong*.

Paulsen published his most successful book yet in 1984. *Tracker* is the story of a teen boy who goes deer hunting while his grandfather is dying. The boy learns about himself and life while out in nature in a difficult situation. The book earned Paulsen a **Society of Midland Authors Book Award**.

HATCHET

Nature had long played a major role in Paulsen's life. For many years, a story had been in the back of his mind. It was a story of survival in the wilderness.

As Paulsen got busy writing, the idea became the story of 13-year-old Brian Robeson. Brian is the sole survivor of a plane crash in the Canadian wilderness. He has only a hatchet to survive alone in the wild for 54 days.

Hatchet hit the bookstores in 1987. The book has sold millions of copies since then. It also inspired several more books about Brian. Plus, *Hatchet* earned Paulsen a **Newbery Honor** award.

The success of *Hatchet* changed things for the Paulsen family. They had a washer and dryer and new furniture for the first time. Paulsen sold his sled dogs to focus more on writing. Ruth used an older barn as her art studio. She contributed illustrations to several of her husband's books.

Paulsen's success also resulted in him adding more tours to his schedule. Paulsen regularly spoke at schools and libraries around the country. At the same time, he continued writing an amazing number of books, both fiction and nonfiction. He also continued his own adventures, whether on a motorcycle, a sailboat, or a horse.

Paulsen won the 1988 Newbery Honor award for **Hatchet.** *He also won the award in 1986 for* **Dogsong** *and 1990 for* **The Winter Room.**

The Stories Continue

In 2012, Paulsen started a new adventure with his son Jim. They decided to write a book. It involved many phone calls and e-mails. Paulsen wrote his parts from his home, which was in New Mexico. Jim, a sculptor, wrote his parts from his home in Minnesota. *Road Trip* is about a father and son on a mission to save a border collie.

The book focuses on dogs, which have always been important to Paulsen. He says dogs saved his life twice. Once, his sled dog Cookie pulled him out of the water after he fell through the ice. Another time, a border collie helped Paulsen when he was pinned under a horse.

Today, Paulsen runs a ranch in New Mexico. He sails his boat around the Pacific Ocean. And, he enjoys riding motorcycles across the American West.

Since the 1990s, Paulsen has focused most of his efforts on young readers. He appreciates how they can be fascinated by a great book. And those are the books he wants to write.

Paulsen enjoys talking with his young readers.

Paulsen is passionate about writing. He likes to dive into his projects. When he writes something that works, he says it makes the hairs on the back of his neck stand up.

Paulsen never plans to retire. That is because he says he can never not write. No matter where his adventures take him, Paulsen's readers can expect a thrilling tale!

GLOSSARY

aerospace (EHR-oh-spays) - the space containing Earth's atmosphere and beyond. It is where rockets, satellites, and other spacecraft operate.

ammunition - bullets, shells, cartridges, or other items used in firearms.

debt (DEHT) - something owed to someone, especially money.

extra - a person hired to act in a group scene in a movie or a play.

immigrant - a person who enters another country to live.

libel - a published false statement that is damaging to a person's reputation.

musher - a person who drives a dogsled.

Newbery Honor - an award given to a runner-up to the Newbery Medal. The Newbery Medal is an annual award given by the American Library Association. It honors the author of the best American children's book published in the previous year.

Oregon Trail - a route across the central and western United States that was used by settlers moving west.

résumé (REH-zuh-may) - a short document that describes a person's education and work history.

Society of Midland Authors Book Award - an annual award that recognizes authors and poets for excellent writing published the previous year.

sue - to bring legal action against a person or an organization.

Vietnam War - from 1957 to 1975. A long, failed attempt by the United States to stop North Vietnam from taking over South Vietnam.

World War II - from 1939 to 1945, fought in Europe, Asia, and Africa. Great Britain, France, the United States, the Soviet Union, and their allies were on one side. Germany, Italy, Japan, and their allies were on the other side.

WEBSITES

To learn more about Children's Authors, visit **booklinks.abdopublishing.com**. These links are routinely monitored and updated to provide the most current information available.

INDEX